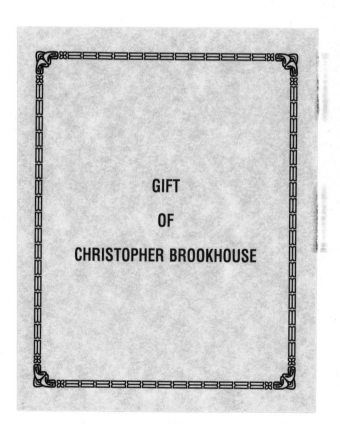

The Descent

Also by Ann Stanford

In Narrow Bound

The White Bird

Magellan:
A Poem to Be Read by Several Voices

The Weathercock

The Descent

Ann Stanford

New York / The Viking Press

First published in 1970 by The Viking Press, Inc.
625 Madison Avenue, New York, N.Y. 10022

Published simultaneously in Canada by
The Macmillan Company of Canada Limited

SBN 670-26705-8

Library of Congress catalog card number: 71-94853

Printed in U.S.A.

Grateful acknowledgement is made for use of poems which previously
appeared in the following books and periodicals: *The Atlantic
Monthly, Chelsea, Coastlines, The Los Angeles Times, The New
Republic, Prairie Schooner, Recurrence, Today's Poets (Chicago
Tribune Sunday Magazine), The Virginia Quarterly Review, The
Western Humanities Review, Yankee;* "Memorial" originally appeared
in *The Massachusetts Review;* "The Committee," "Night of Souls,"
and "The Beating" in *The New Yorker;* and "The Late Visitor,"
"The Descent," "The Voices Inescapable," and "Letter from Portu-
gal" in *The Southern Review.* "The Lecture" appeared in *Themes
and Directions in American Literature: Essays in Honor of Leon
Howard* edited by Ray B. Browne and Donald Pizer. "Cassandra's
Wedding Song" appeared in *High Wedlock Then Be Honoured,*
edited by Virginia Tufte, Copyright © 1969 by Virginia James
Tufte.

I am grateful also to Borestone Mountain Poetry Awards for their selection of "On the Death of the President" for *Best Poems of 1964;* "The Late Visitor" for *Best Poems of 1966;* and "Night of Souls," "To Her Spirit at the Winter Solstice," and "Weeds" for *Best Poems of 1968.*

I wish to thank Evelyn Venable Mohr, Lecturer in Classics at the University of California, Los Angeles, for assistance in the translation from Euripides, and Helen Caldwell, Lecturer in Classics, University of California, Los Angeles, for assistance with the poem "To Carolina," which I translated for inclusion in her book *Machado de Assis: The Brazilian Master and His Novels.* I am grateful also to the Corporation of Yaddo for my residence there during the spring of 1967.

Originals of the paintings and engravings described in "An American Gallery" are to be found as follows: John James Audubon, "The Passenger Pigeon," in *The Birds of America* (1827–1838). William Strickland, "View of Ballston Spa, New York," in the New-York Historical Society, New York. Winslow Homer, "Snap the Whip," in the Metropolitan Museum of Art. Robert Fulton, "Plate the Second," in the New York Public Library. Dolly Hazlewood, Untitled, in the collection of the author. Philip Evergood, "American Tragedy," in the collection of Armand Erpf. Edward Hicks, "The Peaceable Kingdom," in the New York Historical Association, Cooperstown, New York.

To
the long-haired girls
Rosanna   Patricia   Suzy

and to Lois

Contents

I

II

III

[x]

I

By the Woods, Reading

Something is creeping out between the words
The page dawdles its tune
While something slips up behind the wellpoint of the eye

Out there. And the highway roars past the pine trees
The firs that should never have grown there
In the first place. The trucks pass like waves
The old house shakes on their wheels.

But there is something drifting out of the sun
Not the weed puffs that glisten
Or the gnats, wing-caught by the sun.

It has been falling for weeks now.
The slow ash piles round my ankles
Rising from nothing but green—
Or I am sinking in a pond of dandelions.

It is winding between the trees
Tying them together. I am surrounded.
I walk into the dark eye.

The Voices Inescapable

We are never free of the voices.
On waves and wires
Out of the clouds they speak to us.
Wood and steel, nails, bring them through walls.
Edging all buildings, voices mumble their pitch and pause.

Yet down over the rocks of this land
In the undercurrents of the sea
The others are not silent,
Gull and dove,
The coyote over the hills
At night gives us his cry.
Listen to the small voices of the drops of rain now
Settling over us.
The shell whispers back our blood.
The owl tells us at night
Of the soft passers in the leaves.
And the voices from the cloud
Cry: there is no other way.

We will call with the rest for mercy
When the blood
Bludgeons on the carpet,
With the hawk's rabbit
And the raped girl in the forest.

Double Mirror

As this child rests upon my arm
So you encircled me from harm,
And you in turn were held by her
And she by her own comforter.

Enclosed, the double mirror runs
Backward and forward, fire to sun.
And as I watch you die, I hear
A child's farewell in my last ear.

Memorial

I will remember you into light
Or push by thinking into your quiet earth.
I will bring for you this hint of spring
I will think you a black twig with five white blossoms.
Heaven, earth, and man are on this branch.
I will will it to you through the dark
I will press it upon you, a talisman
For your eternity.
Voiceless, in silence, in darkness without sight
How will five blossoms thunder, how bright
Is this black bough, with nodes for shaking green,
Worlds to be born, and all creation burning
In this small bough brought backward into light.

In the Black Forest

Everywhere I go they are coming for me
In the shadow of night
Even through the trees of the Black Forest,
Flying, I suppose, over continents and oceans.

Everywhere I go they find me
And drive up in the old car,
Stepping out, eager to embrace me.
We have not much to say to each other.

But how kind they are to come
Up out of my inner being,
Which they gave and which is really theirs—
And then back to the dark forest and the sea.

2

Gone, gone, but over me still
Broods the winged bird of their spirit
Made of their living breath.
It will last in their children forever.

It covers the bleak sky, a fierce mother—
And from the claws drift down ribbons
Curving scrolls with their mottoes
Which say *Do what you can* and *Take heart*.

[7]

The Fathers

I am beset by spirits, layer on layer
They hover over our sleep in the quilted air.
The owl calls and the spirits hang and listen.
Over our breaths, over our hearts they press.
They are wings and eyes, and they come surely to bless
There is hardly room for the crowd of them under the
    ceiling.

Remember me, remember me, they whisper.

The dark rustles, their faces all are dim.
They know me well, I represent them here.
I keep their lands, their gold and fruiting orchards,
I keep their books, their rings, their testaments.

I am their blood of life made visible
I hold their part of life that vanishes.
They whisper to me, names and messages,
Lost in the world, a sifting down of shadows.

I am myself, I say, it is my blood,
It is my time of sun and lifting of green,
Nothing is here, but what I touch and see.
They cry out *we are here in the root and tree.*
It is my night, I say—and yours for sleeping.
They move their wings, I think I hear them weeping.
Blest spirits, let me be.

And I Came to a Field

There there was a flat stone
  set edgewise.
On one side the words:

     I am myself, nor will I ever be
     A friend to any or an enemy.
     Let them be friend or enemy to me.

     This skull is come, the world to ratify.
     Should any others say *It is*, they lie.
     When it shall pass, then passes earth, all, I.

And on the other side, this rhyme:

     Stanford my father's blood
     Anna my grandmother
     Ann Stanford is my name
     Know me by no other.

Around the thick edge of the stone
from ground to ground
this motto ran:
· FORGET · FORGOTTEN · FORGET · FORGOTTEN ·
  FORGET · FORGOTTEN · FORGOTTEN ·

My house is torn down—
Plaster sifting, the pillars broken,
Beams jagged, the wall crushed by the bulldozer.
The whole roof has fallen
On the hall and the kitchen
The bedrooms, the parlor.

They are trampling the garden—
My mother's lilac, my father's grapevine,
The freesias, the jonquils, the grasses.
Hot asphalt goes down
Over the torn stems, and hardens.

What will they do in springtime
Those bulbs and stems groping upward
That drown in earth under the paving,
Thick with sap, pale in the dark
As they try the unrolling of green.

May they double themselves
Pushing together up to the sunlight,
May they break through the seal stretched above them
Open and flower and cry we are living.

The Given Child

Most lost when found
Most found when lost.
We most must lose
When we love most.

1

In this season comes the child
Out of the black womb.
In this season
Comes the risen god.
In this season
You are born.
In this season lost too.

The sun ranges to the dangerous south
The shortening days speak night to us.
On the turning sun
You enter.

The sun spins in darkness where you grow
Unheeding our voices.

Become in this season yourself.
You do not need us,
Carried in the dark like the sun
To enter and grow like summer.

We gave you life
And that is the great treasure
And now my blood goes circling in the world
I do not know your name.
Henceforth I love all strangers, loving you.
In their young eyes
I see my own reflection.

Unknown child
What was the best?
You take my unpossessing
Everywhere
In a great round of blood, guilt, love.

3

This is the place where there were fields and marshes
And the red-winged blackbirds flew
Up from the rushes.
Olive orchards older than remembering
Covered the hills
And beyond, the orange groves
Dead now, unnatural, bare of leaves.

This cross road I never saw before.

But the hills with the oil wells are the same
Black derricks—and the walking beams
Chug up and down
Where the yellow violets grew in spring.

The jack-rabbit road is straight now
And the trees by my mother's house
Are gone
And the house too and the pond.

We shall leave our bones on the mountain

While it rains, try to find shelter.
If the sun shines, get out of the shadow.
Dry off if you can.
Try to keep going.
If you find berries
The birds have left
Nibble them first.
Grasses are all right to chew.
Be careful of nightshade.

Look for a stream.
Go down beside it.
It will be hard to follow
But if anyone is near at all
They will live by the stream or a bridge will cross it.
Find a road and you may find a cabin.
If they are not there, break in.

It is a long way down.
Don't push too hard.
The bushes will tear at you.

It will be cold where you go.
It will be cold here on the mountain.

The Self Betrayed

Too much was said, or not enough.
And it was late.
But time was the same, lights came and went
Like dawn and dark fastened on one another.
And the flowers had a springing scent.

The guests were statues, and they spoke
From distances.
Since they, or I, were made of stone
I tried to set one voice against the other.
The seraph in the corner was alone.

Behind were doubled up the folded wings.
The hidden sword
That such must carry, shone imperiously—
I saw it catch the garment as it swung.
Yet what I saw I did not seem to see.

And what the figure said I think I know
But in what time or air
Is past remembrance. I saw darkness there
And I spoke loudly, for the darkness hung.
But what I said I cannot seem to hear.

Letter from Portugal

For Barbara—An Elegy

I have come a long way from my country
To find it once more in the clusters of purple
Bougainvillea, hibiscus, the red oleander.
Here grapes too and olives
And oaks on the brown hills.

Autumn in my country, autumn in Portugal
The grapes are purple and red, black are the shadows,
Dry leaves, and the wind blows into the belvederes.
Wind flicks the dry fields over the slopes of the hills
Presses up the undersilver of leaves.

At night the wind brings sounds of children calling
Across the blue cleavings of the sea
Calling *come home, come home.*

—And you in that dark country where you walk
In a dry season, without fountains,
In the color of shade, the rich host of purple
With weighted head by the still river wandering
In that sleeping country,

That was the country that was always yours
To which you always went at evening—
Dark and cool as the shallows of these gardens—

Lost now and listless in the windless darkness
Under the deep pennons of the trees.

Under broad calm, across dull undersea
The children weep. Do you not hear them call—
And move and stir under the heavy shadow—
Come back to us, o prodigal.

Cassandra's Wedding Song

From *The Trojan Women* by Euripides

Hold it up, show it, bring the torch!
I worship with flame.
Look! look!
I light up this holy place!
Hymen, Hymenaeus, Lord!
Blessed the bridegroom
Blessed I too
Whose wedding song leads to the bed
Of a king in Argos.

Seeing that you, mother, can only weep
And lament for the death of my father
And cry out over our loved country,
I must light the fire of the torch
For my own wedding.
To the brightness! to the glory!
I offer to you, O wedding god.
And you, O Hecate, give light
For the marriage bed of a maid, as is the custom.

Whirl, feet high in the air.
Lead on the chorus.
Evan! Evoi!
As when my father's fortune
Was most blessed.

Apollo—thou—
Lead the ritual chorus.
I perform your rites
In your temple among the laurels.

Dance, mother, lead on,
Turn your feet here and there with mine
Carry the sweet steps.
Call out the *Hymen, O*
In happy song
And the shout for the bride.
Come, maidens of Phrygia,
Splendidly dressed
Sing for my wedding
And for the husband
Fate sends to lie beside me.

Mother, crown me with wreaths of victory.
And be glad for this my marriage to a king.
Escort me, and if I seem to you unwilling
Push me away with force. If Apollo lives still
Helen's marriage was not so troublesome
As mine will be to the great Agamemnon.

Mother, there is no need to pity this your land
Nor weep over my marriage. For by this joining
I shall destroy those that both of us hate the most.

   Go now, quickly, that I may quickly wed the
    bridegroom in the house of death.
O leader of the Greeks with
     your haughty vision of great deeds—

Evil man, you will be vilely
                    buried, by night, not in the light of day.

And I—my dead body
                    will be thrown into a gully, naked

Into streams filled by winter rains,
                    close by the grave of the bridegroom

Given to wild beasts to
                    tear to pieces—the servant of Apollo!

I am done with the temple-
                    feasts which were my joy in other days.

Garlands of the god most loved
                    by me, holy ornaments, farewell.

See! I tear them from my body
                    while it is still my own and chaste

And give them to the winds
                    to carry to you, lord of oracles.

Where is the ship of the general?
                    Where must I go to embark?

No longer will you be the
                    first to watch for the wind in the sails

Who take me away from this
                    land—one of the three Avengers.

Say good-bye to me, mother, do not
                    cry. Loved place where I was born

And brothers down there
                    in the earth and father who begot us

Soon you will welcome me.
                    But I shall come to death victorious

Having destroyed the house of
                    Atreus which has ruined us utterly.

The Intruder

There is a cove, hardly visible
coming in from the sea, the sand there warm
the water shallow and clear of wrack—
it drifts in over a ledge and is still.

The dunes are held by flowering vines.
Between them, the sand, smooth, no trace
of footsteps. And near, the laurels
grow down, scattered, to the shore.

The sand nudges up under the cliff
catching the western sun.
One cannot but drowse coming up from the sea
and so I drowsed on sunny afternoons.

Suddenly he had me by the arms—
he had thrown his great spear on the sand
beside his cloak. I called my
father's name: *Nereus! Nereus!*

This stranger with a black beard and strong wrists
keeping me from the water's edge
and my sisters' voices. I became a tree—
stiff bark guarded my thighs, my hands were leaves.

Still he held on. The leaves became
grey feathers and my rooted feet

rose gently as I lifted into flight,
a gull crying out against him.

I tried to lift my wings, but still
he held on, only shifting his weight.
And then I, a tiger, my claws hidden, hard
under the skin. I growled my threat.

Still there, hanging on, though his face
paled. I became the wind and whispered
and fire and burned him
and water—a stubborn man.

One gets tired finally of disguises,
these changing faces. I became
Thetis again and will perhaps remain.
And he, beside me always, a presence.

To Carolina

From the Portuguese of Machado DeAssis

Beloved, to the marriage bed, the last
On which you rest from that far life,
I come, and I shall come, poor dearest,
To bring you the heart of a companion.

There beats in it true affection
Which in spite of all human troubles
Made our life worth desiring
And set a whole world in one dark corner.

I bring you flowers—remains torn by force
From the earth which watched us pass together
And now leaves us dead and apart.

And I, if my eyes, mortally wounded,
Hold thoughts rising up out of life
They are thoughts of what once lived and has ended.

II

Before

When I lay in my mother's womb
Her heart boomed in the chamber above me
The great clock.
Since then I have been enamored of time
And rivers too and seas
Like the sea in which I floated.

The Flood

When I sat beside the river
Thinking of waves higher than buildings
Waves descending like barges down the smooth channel
I thought I dreamed.

But the water came high—
It filled the cellar
Covered grandmother's canned pears
And the quilts by the fireplace.

It rose above grandfather's portrait
Lapped at our feet on the second story.
We looked down the stairs.
Would the house hold?

Could we float on that Ark
Through the corn fields
Downtown past the first national bank
And Gluth's grocery store?

Logs and fence posts piled up by the house.
The pigs flowed away, complaining.
Night was coming down,
The waters pushed at the foundations,
Our dog whined in the upstairs bedroom.

What could we do but sit there?
We made a raft of the bedstead
And a plank off the bedroom dresser.
We were ready to knock a hole in the wall
For launching. But the stream began to go down.

It went down to mud. The crops were gone,
The animals lost or dead. But we were alive.
The old house as good a ship as any.
Whenever I look at the river
I think of those waves and wonder.

Night Rain

I wake with the rain.
It has surprised me.
First, delight,
Then I think of outdoors:
The shovels and rakes I left in the garden
Rusting now in the mist,
The splintering of handles.
I think of car windows open
Tricycles
Canvas cots, trash cans
The hay uncovered
Mildew.

Well, they are out.
And the animals—
The cat, he is gone
The dog is the neighbor's
The horses have a tin roof
If they will stay under it.
And the wild things are there—
Birds, wet in the trees,
Deer in the brush, rabbits in hiding.
The leaves will all be washed
The wild lilacs, the walnuts.

I am sleepy and warm
I dream of the great hornéd owl
Snatching birds like plums out of trees.

The Arrayal

What did she wear when she searched through the bureau
  drawer
Under the rectangle of handkerchiefs
Pushing under the socks
And her father's cuff-links and coins?

What did she choose for the walking into the yard
The square of lawn between the hydrangea and apricot,
Stepping over the pool in the grass by the leaky hose,
Patting her hair that was blown by the little wind?

Did she wear the gold necklace of her mother
And the pale linen dress ready for summer
When she opened the doors of her body
And the red foam flicked in the sunlight?

The Beating

The first blow caught me sideways, my jaw
Shifted. The second beat my skull against my
Brain. I raised my arm against the third.
Downward my wrist fell crooked. But the sliding

Flood of sense across the ribs caught in
My lungs. I fell for a long time,
One knee bending. The fourth blow balanced me.
I doubled at the kick against my belly.

The fifth was light. I hardly felt the
Sting. And down, breaking against my side, my
Thighs, my head. My eyes burst closed, my
Mouth the thick blood curds moved through. There

Were no more lights. I was flying. The
Wind, the place I lay, the silence.
My call came to a groan. Hands touched
My wrist. Disappeared. Something fell over me.

Now this white room tortures my eye.
The bed too soft to hold my breath,
Slung in plaster, caged in wood.
Shapes surround me.

No blow! No blow!
They only ask the thing I turn
Inside the black ball of my mind,
The one white thought.

The Friend

I lay upon the ice in day.
The wind shook with the cold. A lumpy plain
All white lay round me. At the edge of the sky
A mass of ice pushed up a jagged hill

Ribbed like a mountain layered with shale.
I wished to die, but my impounded blood
Ran warm and thoughtful through the narrow pulse.
I rose upon it, held by its moving streams.

All round, the ice. Far off, white and chill,
Water shone next the mound of grey.
My feet slipped as I trod ghostly to that hill.
My hands froze as I climbed by block and crack.

And from the top, glare shown at me.
No thing moved there, the wind gnawed nothing.
Till at last a wisp, pale on the sky
In the far broken plain, a thought of smoke.

Then I bent slowly to the house
All snow encrusted next a cliff of ice.
The door moved at a touch, the warmth flowed round
The small room furnished with a failing fire.

No sound. But on the table there
The tea still warm, a cup not empty yet,
But cold, and the fire just winking out.
I knew he would not turn back to that room.

The Escape

The walls were close enough to reach between
They were of brick and they were slanting in.
I held them up—one foot, two arms, my head.

I held for hours. When I stirred, they leaned.
They trembled with my breath but did not fall.
I shifted feet, my arms were numb.

My head ached with the flatness of the wall.
I saw my foot set on the concrete ground.
A spider crawled from one wall to the other.

Nothing else moved.   I could hold no longer.
I took my foot down. Carefully one hand
And then the other, I drew gently down

And lifted up my head and saw a door
And I went out and breathed under the trees.
I looked back at the walls. They stood alone

A cubicle of dryness on the lawn.
I watched the slow dust as they toppled one by one.

On the Way

The day after Christmas. Everything is clean
And bright by rains, the leaves on the acacias
And toyon. Stopped up the hill I can see

The mountains, gray with gashes of snow
And the ocean glaring in the sun.
I could see boats if there were any.

But the sea is a clear table top.
I go down the hill. Things glisten. The clouds
Are clean-edged on painted blue.

Down by the boulevard the palm trees
Are having their fronds cut. They drop
From the heads of the stolid date palms

And the thin cocos a hundred feet high.
A man in a crow's nest on top of a crane
On top of a truck is doing the job.

Fronds fall, missing the man in the turtle-neck
Sweater and the woman in the leopard coat
Who wait for the bus. Roses—notice: don't pick—bloom in
    the park.

[35]

I pass Gogian's Tire Honesty and the tracks
Where I have never seen a train. Fat pigeons
Are grazing on the grass between the ties.

Three men are coming home from the moon.
Carloads of skiers go off to the mountains.
This hour's all I count on.

The Committee

Black and serious, they are dropping down one by one to
the top of the walnut tree.
It is spring and the bare branches are right for a conversa-
tion.
The sap has not risen yet, but those branches will always be
bare
Up there, crooked with ebbed life lost now, like a legal
argument.
They shift a bit as they settle into place.
Once in a while one says something, but the answer is always
the same,
The question is too—it is all *caw* and *caw*.
Do they think they are hidden by the green leaves partway
up the branches?
Do they like it up there cocking their heads in the fresh
morning?
One by one they fly off as if to other appointments.
Whatever they did, it must be done all over again.

The Lecture

For Leon Howard

Relaxed at the podium, he finished his apple.
The core crashed the waste can
And just as the bell rang
He began to conjure.

At the other end of the darkness
A hand stirred in its lace and the scattered bodies
Pulled themselves together as for the day of doom.
Edwards outstared the Indians at Stockbridge
Finding that God after all was an aesthete
While Franklin turned his attention to Madame Brillon.
There were no sluggards in the tale; the hour was never too
   long.
Barlow, defining equality
Hurried after Napoleon over the snow.
In the snow of Pittsfield Melville tossed on the sea
And sighted the drifting of an ambiguous whiteness.

"Strike through the mask," he cried, just short of the hour.
And the stone heart warmed in two hundred breasts
And the dark blood seeped up from under Hawthorne's
   leaves.

An American Gallery

JOHN JAMES AUDUBON
"The Passenger Pigeon"
Hand-colored engraving

Real as any other birds you sit in the maple.
Your cry—what is it?—descends on evening fields—
or morning—your red feet
indent our berry patches. Your curved beak
pocks the ripe sides of our peaches.
Vagabond, useless—your bright eye
searches for seedlings, fresh cotyledon leaves.
You ravage our fields with your out-of-season
perpetual appetite.

Villain, we have shot at you
your numberless progeny that blacken our skies.
Plague, feathered locusts,
filling our woods with your coos and caws.
Out of the north you come in endless clouds
harder than hail you descend on the harvest.

Wonder! to have caught so few here—
only two on a branch mottled with lichen
beside three dead leaves. Thieves!

We might think you were numbered
or that your days might end.

WILLIAM STRICKLAND
"View of Ballston Spa, New York"
Water color, c. 1794

A plague has overwhelmed this forest.
The boles of trees lie across one another.
Those standing are dead, their branches cracking.
From some the tops have fallen—all are bare
except for one in the fore, still yellow and dying.

The small men with axes
have girdled them as far as the horizon.
The stumps have been hacked. They resemble
the stubs of torsos.

This was a forest of firs.
The eight men moving like pygmies
among the roots of the tall trees
have put up the four white buildings.
They have placed porches in front, and balconies,
dreaming of prospect: smooth lawns and
Roman goddesses welling up out of fountains.
A small shed roof covers the rising water.

A forest is being burned outside the picture.
The smoke is rolling over Ballston Spa.

WINSLOW HOMER
"Snap the Whip"
Oil on canvas, 1872

Eight boys in a rocky meadow,
sired just before the drums rolled at Shiloh,
their pants turned up above their ankles—
one, larger than the rest, has outgrown his.
Some are patched at the knees.
They all wear suspenders.

Their shirts—long-sleeved, or hidden under their coats—
were made at home by their mothers or
sisters sitting by coal-oil lamps.
They have hats or caps just shading their eyes.
Five are barefoot; three are wearing shoes.

We see by this that it is an indefinite season.
Spring has put forth the grass
and brought the sun down upon them,
but there are clouds, they are dark under—
it may just have rained. There are flowers,
indistinguishable bits of blue and yellow.

They play in a clearing, the woods behind them,
and in the foreground the tangle
of flowers and red leaves—the new leaves of sumac?
The wood is encroaching—two small trees
threaten the turf where they are playing.

The building behind them—a square
too small for a house. Around it

the grass is packed into ground. Outside each window
shutters hang open on the red wall. The sash
is partly lifted to the new spring air.

Why are they here, so far from the village?
You can see the white steeple off in the distance,
a few white buildings all but hidden in trees.
In between, a ploughed field and two barns
or a house and a barn. Where are their fathers?

The boys play hard. The pivot leans backward
holding the center while the others run past
and the boy at the end tumbles on hands and knees.
Their faces are serious. The third boy is shouting.
No one listens. They are rousing boys,
school is out for the day, the trees are green, summer is
    coming.

ROBERT FULTON

"Plate the Second'
Water color, 1804

This cross section, here incorrectly titled
"Mechanical Drawing for a Steamboat,"
is not a steamboat at all.
This is part of a submarine.

Note how at Valve A the water
is pouring in. The deck just skims
above the water line outside.
Inside, the water surrounds

A cylinder. This is the core
of the boat. Its sides, one inch thick,
can stand pressures to one hundred
perpendicular feet of water.

Six men can enter the core
through the hatch at the top.
And men, turning a handle,
turn the screw that drives the vessel.

Between Deck B and the upper deck
on both sides of the boat the inventor
has neatly spelled out its purpose.
It has "Chambers for Submarine Bombs."

This ship can surface by day. By night
it can submerge and enter a harbor

and its bombs, left anchored or floating,
will destroy whatever passes.

This plate depicts a practical
submersible ship. Robert Fulton
praised it as an instrument
for true liberty and peace.

DOLLY HAZLEWOOD
Untitled
Oil, c. 1940

The peach orchard faces the woods
And in between
Runs a narrow of bluebonnets.

The peach trees slant down a hill
Pungent with bloom
And are caught against a rock wall.

The wall is the only sign of man
And it seems fallen.
The picture is a celebration of spring

In which between the woods and the orchard
Bluebonnets cover the earth
And tint every hill under the sky.

Could the artist be saying that man's
Works are succumbing to nature?
Or that in between

Nature and art is the place for bluebonnets?
Or did she on that heart-full morning
Simply frame the best view of her flowers?

Great Aunt Doll was a woman of spirit.
When she died at last in a sanitarium
She was making a vast collection of seashells.

PHILIP EVERGOOD

"American Tragedy"

Oil on canvas, 1937

South of Chicago, the black chimneys of the steel mills
are soiling the sky. Their walls are red. No one is near them.
But there is action aplenty. A corps of policemen
armed with night-sticks and guns
are beating the fleeing citizens.

The night-sticks are raised and fall with equal pity
on men and women, fair-skinned and dark.
They rain on the shirt-sleeved men and the women in sum-
    mer dresses.
A man falls backward, his chin thrown up by a fist.
An Italian clutches his chest where a bullet has found him.

Those who can are running away.
A black man lies on his face, blood falls from his mouth.
He holds in his hand the flag of the land of the free.
None shall escape, the policemen work hard.
They are shooting the blonde woman in the pink dress

While she, her hands empty, held high, runs from
that blue army. In the center a man holds back the police
    with his hand,
his arm is around the Mexican woman in green.
Her fist is clenched, she holds a stick as weapon.
She is pregnant. A club hangs over this man's head.

The red of the wall of the mill colors the scene.
It drips from the brow of the man who has lost his straw hat,

[46]

from the mouth of the black man, from the chest of the
  other.
It will break from the heads of the red-headed man
And the woman in green. Puddles, bright as blood
Or the melting pots of the mills, color the streets of the city.

EDWARD HICKS
"The Peaceable Kingdom"
Oil on wood, c. 1830

This was the peaceable kingdom: the river flows
like time beside it. This tiny slope,
grass covered, slants up to an impassable forest.

Half up the sky a natural bridge
curves like a rainbow. In such a place
Penn pledged his peace to all his Indian brothers.

He stands there, engraved, given to fat,
his friendly hands extended to the natives
who, lean as Caesar, accept his fatal gifts.

But that good Quaker in his peaceful country
is past and backdrop. On this crowded shore
herded together, the wolf and the lamb lie down

And the tiger looks at the kid as once
in the garden of Eden, innocent of blood.
The calf, the young lion, the fatling lie together.

And the cow and the bear share their ration of straw,
The lion and the ox beside one another, surprised.
The eagle and dove eat from the hands of a child.

Another plays with the serpent. In all this mountain
there is no danger, for the earth is filled
with the word of the lord. There is no hunger.

[48]

How could this be? Even here, withdrawn on a mountain,
where the quail and dove walk at the grasses' edges,
I hear the world washing away my kingdom.
The deer go by, seeking the last wild ranges.

On the Death of the President

November 22, 1963

In a current of eagles and parks and green,
In a blue ripple of shouts, in the hearty sun,
The day moves with autumn and feasting,
Cheers, and the rustle of crowds, and the held faces.

Stretched beyond the green savannahs of our knowing
Deep in marshes and trees, in scrub oak, the deer
Stands flicking his shoulders, dappled in shade.
The dogs scare up the autumn colors of partridge.

The world centers on noon, the White Mountains have
    passed it,
The Rockies still hold morning's sun on the early snow.
In the Cascades the spruces cast their shadows westward.
The country gathers toward noon in the midst of the coun-
    try.

Into the forest of our knowing, across the marked paths,
Over the billow of flags and the hails and the shot,
Beneath the crowd's crumpled breath,
Hunted and fallen, the fated and noontime meet.

Noon turns suddenly black, and the sigh falls over
The sun like the shadow of all the mists of breath,
Like a prayer tears fall among the avenues,
The noon's huge sun wrapped in the mists of mourning.

Through the long afternoon a coffin rides the skies
Death flies above, the air weeps at his passing,
Awake we dream out woe, the day curves on,
Earthbound, we walk through autumn bells and harvests.

In afternoon's fields we gather, we gather in folds
And all the flowers are garnered and gathered
In the mountains, in the fields and towns, under the pine
    trees:
Goldenrod, firethorn, buckwheat, red-leaved sumac.

Into the soft-leaved evening we wait and the flight is ended.
End and beginning and end, forever and ever.
The dead and the living
Enter the darkening field—and each to his fortune.

While the dark with its loss falls over the capital
And seeps over the Potomac into the fields of Arlington
And spreads over West Virginia and the Appalachians
And drops over the great plains of the Mississippi
Engulfs the Bad Lands and the Black Hills
And creeps slowly up over Santa Fé and the Sangre de
    Cristo
Over the Wind River and the Great Basin and the Mojave
And high, high over the Sierra Nevada—without a star—
And drifts down over the calm Pacific.

The Speed of Planes

They have been falling from the sky
Ever since they went there
And the two wings, upper and lower,
Were stretched, catching the wind
Straining upward, a kite
To the sun. The wings have changed us.

> Noisy and hurrying we forget
> To listen, we forget the wind
> That once said winter is coming,
> We forget the walking on the earth,
> We forget the midnight message
> And the slow drifting of small things.

Till in the offering of fire
We have poured our children.
We heard them laughing together
While the planes hurled overhead.
We heard all turn to silence
In the building of the flame.

From the Air

The plane is a dizzy platform
From which to fall
The sea rising, rising
And the earth
Thick, growing green fetters
And its poisonous breed
Serpents, spiders, fierce claws.

The dog, domestic, a sudden wolf,
Snaps at the hand.
At the back the knife.

Time passing, time passing.

The Informer

I am the wind and I am whispering
about you. I am catching them
on corners, saying, saying
I am the wind and I am whispering

Three Poems for a Read-In

1

When the enemy comes, let him drop bombs on your house
Alone. I am too kind-hearted to stick pins in your effigy.
As I pass your house my thumb is turned down
I say *Die! Wither!*

I will plant marijuana in your garden
And then call the local police.
When they come, they will knock you down
And take you to jail for a thousand years.

2

When I woke up
I saw justice blindfolded
and she held a balance—
in one pan was a fish
its eyes glazed with a blue film.
Its gills stood permanently open.
A few scales hung loose from its sides,
the rest shrank together.
It was five days stinking.

[55]

In the other, a turkey, defeathered,
its head hanging limp,
swayed in the air.
Its claws clutched upward.

The balance in one hand,
She had me in the other.
"Which will you go against?" she said.
"Fish or turkey
you are done for,"
cried the blind hag laughing.

3

The reason I have not killed myself
Is I have too many letters to answer.
The bills must be paid
The drawers cleaned out
And the old clothes packed in paper bags
For the Good Will.
The book must be finished
Letters given to libraries
Mementoes assigned to the proper kin
And the children remembered
By various sums.
It will take a lifetime to do this.

III

A Discourse

From the *Bhagavad Gita*

The Lord said:

I am the self
That lies in the heart of all creatures.
I am the beginning
The enduring and the end of all.

Of the sons of space, I am Vishnu
Of heavenly lights, I am the sun
I am the chief among the gods of storm
I am the moon shining among stars.

Of Vedas, I am the book of chants
Of gods, I am Indra, lord of the air
I am the mind among the senses
I am awareness in living things.

Of the terrible gods, I am Shiva
Of sprites and demons I am lord of wealth
Among the bright ones I am lord of fire
I am the mountain where the gods abide.

I am Prahlada, prince of Titans
I am time itself among the hours
I am king of the beasts of the forest
I am Lord of the Sky, the bird of Vishnu.

I am the purifier, god of wind
Rama among bearers of weapons
I am the sea-monster among fishes
Ganges among the rivers.

I am the beginning and the end
And the middle of all creations
I am the knowledge of the soul.
I am the discourse of those who speak.

I am the letter A
And the coupling of compounds.
I am time inexhaustible
And the creator, facing everywhere.

I am death who harries all
The rising up of what will be
Of months, first, when the moon enters the Deer,
Of seasons, the flower-abounding.

I am the gambling of the cheat
The sharp edge of the brilliant.
I am victory. I am effort.
I am courage to the stout-hearted.

I am the rod of the master
The statecraft of those who seek conquest
I am the silence of secret things
The knowledge of them that know.

And whatever is the seed of all beings
That I am also.

No creature that moves or does not move
Could exist without me.

Whatever creature comes forth in glory
In vigor and in beauty
Know that that being has sprung
From but a fragment of my splendor

Or rather—for what to you
Is such a multitude of knowing?—
I stand and hold up this universe
With a single portion of myself.

Arjuna said:

It is proper, Lord, that praising you
The world exults and is tinged with your colors.
Demons, afraid, flee to all quarters
And throngs of perfect souls do homage.

And why should they not revere you, Great-souled?
Older than Brahma, you are the first creator.
Endless, lord of gods, the world's home,
You are eternal, what is and is not, and beyond.

You are the primal god, the ancient person,
In you all things come down to rest,
Knower and known, you are the highest power.
From you comes all, Unending Form.

God of wind, moon, fire, all-holding sky
Lord of death, Maker, Father of all,

Glory, glory to you a thousandfold
And to you be glory, glory still.

Glory to you, before and after,
And on all sides, All, glory to you.
You of endless strength, unmeasured in power
You pervade all things. You are all, therefore.

What I said roughly, thinking you comrade,
Saying Krishna, Son of Yadu, O friend,
In sport or by way of affection
Not knowing this your greatness—

If I joked and tormented you
While we played or ate or sat resting
By ourselves or with the others, O Unshaken,
Unbounded, forgive me.

Father of all that moves and is still,
We honor you, the greatest worthy.
In the three worlds there is none like you.
Supreme Power, who could be more?

Therefore I bow and bend down before you.
Be gracious, lord to be praised.
As father to son, friend to friend,
Lover to loved, be gentle, O God.

The Descent

Let us, therefore, bend all our force and thoughts of
soul to this most holy light, that showeth us the way
which leadeth to heaven; and after it, putting off the
affections we were clad withal at our coming down, let
us clime up the stairs which at the lowermost step have
the shadow of sensual beauty, to the high mansion-place
where the heavenly, amiable, and right beauty dwelleth.

—BALDASSARE CASTIGLIONE

As I descend from ideal to actual touch
As I trade all the golden angel crowns
And rings of light for gross engrossing sense,
As I descend Plotinus' stairs,
Angel, man, beast, but not yet plant and stone,
The sense of that height clings, the earthen hand

Transmutes again to light, is blessed from black
Through alchemy to rise rich red, green, blue,
Fractions of vision broke from ample crowns.

As I from the mind's distance fall on voyages
I test the strength of water where I walk
And lose the air for wings. I am lifted
As I descend past clouds and gusts of air
As I go down with wind to tops of trees
As I walk down from mountain tops and cold.

As I descend to gardens warm with leaves
As I enter the new morning harsh in sun
I count the earth with all its destinies
Come down to prove what idea does not know.

[63]

I descended out of nothing into green
I descended out of spaces where the spare
Stepping stones of islands roughed my way.
I descended into solidness, to dense
And mingled shrubberies where the birds
Alone choose wings for crossing my old sky.

Caught in this day within a sound of hours
Walled into shadows, stripped of multitudes,
I try this spring the growing into light.

In the Husk

In the darkness of this womb
Or this winding
Done up in cords spun
Out of myself
I wait.

There was light
And I consumed
Husks, leaves, veins
Drinking the sap
Turning the long pith
Into silk
That now enfolds me.

It is at last this darkness
That I have come to
Tired of moving about
Of lifting the head
And the searching feet
Set carefully among the branches.

I am shaken down
Falling into my silken dream.

O this dark dark winding into the dark
Immobile, insignificant
Self-tied, self-prisoner
Not dead, not living, but moving on
To the new air I have not yet conceived.

By the Waters

The dew invites me
And the fog that rides
The nights of spring.
Rain and rivers tug,
And fountains in the sun
Catch up my steps and run
Through pools and channels
And I am caught in spray.

Willing and unwilling is the way
My feet are drawn
Down with the stream
To the last firm of earth,
There to hold
By the paused oceanswell—
While the sea sucks back its ravel
And grows and hovers—and not blench aside,
But stung with reason speak
To subjugate this tide.

The Rod

Impero igitur tibi ne in terram meam ascendas, nec vestes neo membra dominatoris tui madefacere praesumas.

—CANUTE

I have beat back the waters.

Here the rod
That follows on those undulant pursuers
To downward rocks and silence of the dense
Concentric whorls of motion's central core.

Whence to return
They first must coil and restless set their round
Against the deepest sounding
That presses black and turns itself to stone.

Rigid and yet
      In stillness burning.

The sea is gone and shining is the sand
The sand is smooth, the paving of the sea.
And round and gaping creatures lie aground.

The rod is made of light.
It is a crystal and imperial thing.
Far, far, the waves depart beyond its bend.
It is the lasting day that circumvents all night.
It is the light.

Light that revolves against the sleepless eye,
Divides in suns and glaring galaxies.

Who looks at sun grows blind at what he sees

And calls on black and calls on dark to turn.

O blessed seas that in your dark uncoil
And throw your serpent clouds upon the sky
That thundering return across the grey
And empty sea-plain, catching up the dry

And hollowed creatures, curving in the sun.
O blessed dark that runs across the day
That opens caverns precious to the sight
Of censured vision that in depth delights.

I hear your roar returning up the sand
I feel your constant pulse beneath the shore
I see the rocks impatient for your streams.

And watch the rod descend into your brim.
Then come notorious day and spend your beams

And fall to sea and night.

The Organization of Space

1

Vacancy goes with me as does a sea,
Perfect, round, in all directions sending
All the not-where, where that one is not bending,

Or the wide disk of grain, shadeless of trees,
Empty, and the arch empty, of seeing,
Above, below, unconscious of that being,

And the great desert parched of all—
No rock, no shadow—without green or air—
Only salt and dry, that center being not there.

2

Add to the dull disk of sea, colors of coral,
A speck of land within brief shafts of water—
Then we have distance and before and after.

Set in the midst of grain a single tree
And like a magnet pulling into place,
It draws a path across the unlined space.

And in the desert the uprising stone
Cuts into space and makes the skies convene.
Landmarks arise, and in the shade a green.

3

I praise a local vista, clipped or rough.
It makes its variants with sun and frost—
Hill, row, and field—till vacantness is lost.

And from such centering, the wires that join
The farm and town, the seen and unseen line
Can mark out waves' and gravity's design.

Arched like a row of tents with canvas seams,
The sky is propped by pole and spire to show
They hold the circles fixed through which I go.

4

And yet a vacancy, an almost none,
An arching of the mind into a sky
Under which empty fields and barrens lie,

A round of almost gone, a black and sere,
Returns across the vivid local tiers
And turns them to a round, unshaded sea.

Spirit or being, corn-god or harvester,
That sets us deep within the year's concern,
Hold the circumference in which we turn.

In the Lenten Season

Risen, the masquerade of flesh
Compounds this floating spring, the plane
Of trees, bloom, terrace, where we pass
The garrulous afternoon. The noun

Is what is feared: to name the sly
Commotion of the blood which runs
Unplanned as leaves to their own ways.
The day ends in a double vision

Of the self immaculate, and its brood
Of interior dwellers—kernel and shell:
The token ritual, grown hard,
And the sweet corruptible.

The Late Visitor

Listen, let me explain, it was not the fire
That burned in the hearth and kept me there.
It was no real fire, though I swear it did seem so
And to go out was to step into blackest snow,
And to stay was to lose, not find. Words only say
What is gone. Or are motions like flame and snow,
Slow circlings of something about to occur,
The birth of a salamander in the fire.

I am caught between never and now. You must tell me to go.

The Gift

It was round, orb being most nearly perfect,
And warm perhaps, though hardly of any color,
Smelling of spring, faintly, of hyacinth.
It was not fruit, though on those trees first planted
Eastward, of life and knowledge, it may have grown.
There were many trees in Eden. And this not eaten.
Yet flower neither, though soft as petals
Yet harder perhaps, like pearls hunted
Through dark shore-caves, or rubies hidden,
Precious as those, glanced at and not seen.
Transparent, then, and gone like water
Floating off, yet here; and single, out of many,
And not illusion, though it may have been.
Solid and constant, ephemeral and shaken,
Fruit, flower, or stone, or given or taken.

Morning

From the center of our body
Come the bright flowers.

Draw open the curtain
And we shall see them
On bush and stone.

Let us exchange our borders
That I may speak with your voice.

Mirror

In this mirror your face is broken
The sockets of your eyes
Cleave from the cheeks
And the smile pulls
Half a face.
There is a wen behind your ear
And the knuckles of your hands
Grow large.
Your skin is withered.
Your hand shakes.
I loved you.
I am lost.

Postcard from Venice

This city is floating away on the sea
The sea is holding it up, taking it south
The sea is bursting up between the pavings
Froth is moving it seaward.

This city is being carried away
It is flying.
There are angels lifting St. Mark's with their pinions
The lion is bearing his post, the saints ride their pillars
The gods on the cornice are hoisting it higher.

Wings and the sea are tossing the city.
The wind is pushing it up to the rooftops
The angels are taking it over the Alps
Suspended in water and clouds, floating and flying.

A Birthday

On the morning of my birthday I awoke from a dream
Where I came down from walking in a park on a hill.
The hill had two sides: on one the bright chaparral
Stood separate and shining on the brown hay of summer
On the other, pineshade—and ferns on the floor of a forest.
They vanish away as smoke in the air.

The ground was soft underfoot
It was evenly planted; all things were in order.
I was barefoot, and it was holiday
And I came down and found the streets full of people
And I walked in full and swinging skirts among them.
He is great that sets at nought all worldly honor.

Beloved, we go west to the wide sea
All of us, coming down from the hill.
All of us, all, borne on the shell of earth—
Though far from the sea you ride.
And I may behold all things as they be, of short abiding.

At my center is a pool, calm
Dark. I have not found its edges.
And as I turn westward
Though I have not found wisdom

The great pool of peace is the center, what I am and that
   only.
May nothing take from thee inward liberty of soul.

In this first morning of my year I awoke
And all things were hung with light.

Night of Souls

I saw each soul as light, each single body
With his life's breath kindled and set like flame
Before his nostrils. All creatures visible—
Small beings moving in the midnight grasses,

Light in the thoroughfares underfoot
The mole's house hung with the mole's breath
As with candles, and the busy air
Clouded with light.

It is no longer midnight, for the sea
Rustles translucent waters, windows letting out
The glow of all its denizens, colored as through
Cathedral glass, the night sky dark
Save where a lost gull drops like a meteor
Into the phosphorous waves.

The linnets chirp as in daylight. The owl dazzles himself.
Silent and still, wondering by the glare of his mother
The new colt shines.
Light betrays the young deer in the thicket

On this night of the lighting of spirits
All quiet, all visible
Till the lantern of man comes up over the hill,
Shades out those other beams like a bare sun rising.

Numbers

When we think of numbers, they are what move
In the wind, over the ground, through the thick seines
Of water. Small. They rustle around us.

Or silent. What can't be counted. I have seen
A hive of bees hang on a branch of our lilac
The wild thorny blue of the endless blossoms.

Now in autumn here the leaves turn from numbers
Become mass where the wild walnuts
Plan now the deluge of spring from the ends

Of the dying branches. And the meek, and grass,
Move toward inheritance. New fish in the streams.
I have dreams beyond count and remember.

Going Away

The horses are going away
The tall mare and the four-year-old.
Their bridles lie by the drive,
And their gear and what is left of the oats.

They do not know. They are out there sleeping.
Over them the tin roof bangs in the wind.

They will wade into acres of grass
And hear the new sound of a sea
That breaks past the hill and the steady branches of oaks
In a place where the roads have not come yet.

How they will run in the big pasture
Or stand, flicking their tails in the sunlight
Those high beasts that looked over our shoulders
Or stood silent, nuzzling, blocking the way.

They called to us when we were slow at evening.
The young one was born here.

We will go back into our houses
We will forget how large the world was once.

To Her Spirit
at the Winter Solstice

Now the year ends darkly.
The sun drifts in the south.
Will it ever return?

And you force me in the cold to gather red berries
Up early in mist, breaking the branches—
The musky smell of the toyon—
Will this be enough?

Look down, spirit, from your height of fire,
Look from the skiff crossing the black river.
Call back the sun that lingers.

Shall I bring only remembering
Who cannot bring flowers? for the cold
Grows deep and dark where you linger.

And the ship of fire goes farther
Toward some chill cape of waves and darkness.
Hold fast in the rough riding.

O blown spirit, do not draw me
To those chill tides
Where I too cast my offerings
In darkness.

Weeds

Nothing so startles us as tumbleweeds in December
Rising like ghosts before us in the headlamps
The big round weeds blowing into fences
Into guard rails and wheels, wedged into corners
Drifting in ranks over roads in a gusty order
Round in the orbits of winter, dropping the invisible seed,
Blown green and purple-leaved into springtime, soft with
    water,
Filled to harsh circles in the thirsty summer
Dried brown and jagged, ready for December
When the silver globes, magnificent in procession
Slow and solemn-paced in the ritual of ending
Dry, dead, in the dim-most part of the year
Spread the great round promises of green morning.